Global warming, or the greenh
the greatest environmental pro
face over the next fifty years. "
and oil, the destruction of the rainforest, the release
of methane and nitrous oxide from agriculture, and
the use of heat-trapping CFCs are all raising the
temperature of our planet. It is now estimated that
by 2040 the Earth may be hotter than at any time
during the last 120,000 years.

The implications of such rapid climate change are
grave. Rising sea levels will cause flooding and
homelessness, more frequent hurricanes and
typhoons will bring devastation, and disruption of
crop-growing and food supply will mean hunger
for many.

In this clear and detailed book, Mary and John
Gribbin look at the causes and threats of the growing
greenhouse effect and suggest steps which
individuals and governments can take to protect the
Earth for future generations.

Mary Gribbin has a degree in developmental psychology and works as a special needs teacher in primary education. She has written several books on science topics for young readers.

John Gribbin has a degree in physics and works as a science writer with a special interest in global environmental issues. He has written several books on science topics for older readers.

The greenhouse tim

By Steve Connor
Science Correspondent

THE SCIENTISTS whose report prompted Margaret Thatcher's speech on global warming last week are now more convinced the problem is more urgent and alarming than the bulk of their report suggests, and that both they and the Prime Minister may have underestimated the long-term effects.

A summary of the report by the United Nations Intergovernmental Panel on Climate Change (IPCC) was released on Friday. It forecast a 3C rise in average temperatures and a 65-centimetre rise in sea levels by the end of next century, which led the Prime Minister to call for a "giant international effort" to save the planet.

But scientists who compiled the full report now believe that a complex and little-understood mechanism called "positive feedback" could have an even more radical effect on climatic change. The full text of the 300-page report is still unpublished. A paragraph which refers to this process was inserted into the report, but only at the last minute. The paragraph states: "Although many of these feedback processes are poorly understood, it seems likely that, overall, they will act to increase, rather than decrease, greenhouse gas concentrations in a warmer world . . . and hence the climate change would be more rapid than predicted."

Positive feedback occurs when the warmer world created by the emission of man-made gases itself causes further warming. Some of these processes could cause a rapid and sudden acceleration in global warming. For example, scientists believe that the melting of the polar ice sheet, caused by a warmer world, would uncover vast tracts of ocean which would evaporate and thus add significantly to global warming.

Environmental scientists have become increasingly concerned about such mechanisms. Finally, at their meeting at Windsor last week, they agreed that the evidence was so strong it should be included in their final report.

John Woods, direc...

Britain's Natural Environment Research Council, who is a member of the team that produced the UN report, said: "There's a time bomb waiting to go off. How long that will take depends on the accuracy of our models, which are at present not refined enough to say."

Not yet green? 10

Dr Woods criticised governments for failing to improve the system of gathering information on how and when feedback mechanisms will come into effect.

"There is not as yet an ...
intern...

urgent they should do so."

Dr Woods highlighted tw
feedback processes of particula
concern.

■ Presently about a third of the
solar heat trapped in the atmo
sphere by the natural greenhouse
effect finds its way into deep, cold
regions of the ocean, particularly
in the northern part of the North
Atlantic and the oceans off Antarctica. The circulation of surface
water to deep layers transports
the heat to these "sinks".

But, Dr Woods said, a warmer
world would increase rainfall and
more fresh water would run into
the oceans. Circulation of water
ld be disrupted as the salinity
e ocean
norm
wo

GLOBA

UN warns of global timebomb

Paul Brown
Environment Correspondent

CLIMATE change will have devastating effects on millions of people, animals and plants as fer...

report, scientists say adapting will prove impossible in many cases.

Although their findings are provisional, they say the changes will be so rapid in the next 60 years that nature will be unable to adapt, and man will not be able to control them.

Africa will be worst affected, with wood supplies for cooking and deserts ad...

cost $3 billion (£1.8 billio
rectify. In Britain, rainfall
pected to come in sh
sharper bursts, leadi
greater soil erosion and l
and less water filtering t
to top up ground wate
will lead to water sl
each summer.

Air pollution, espe
cities, is expected to g
adversely affectin
Increases in

GLOBA

T

We mus
now to a
this clim
of destru

By
DR JOH
GRIBBI
Award winning
and author of H

AS WE pick up the pi
tain's second hurric
than three years. I
bad news to report
plenty more on the way.

The Greenhouse Effect – t
of global warming – will en
the 1990s will see our tr
weather turned upside down.
start to take action now
the problem can only get
worse.

But the bottom line is
that governments world-
wide must get together to
help ease the conse-
quences.

The problem is that
storms grow where warm
air from the South meets
cold air from the North.

...rs of global warming

bomb

"When that hap-
[...]ll be a rapid accel-
[...]bal heating."

[...]e sheet acts as a bar-
[...] the Arctic Ocean,
[...] at a temperature
[...]zing point, and the
[...] air above, which
[...] 40C colder. As
[...] disappeared, in a
[...], this relatively
[...]uld come into con-
[...]lder air above and
[...]rate quickly.
[...]king the lid of a
[...] water will evapo-
[...]his will produce a
[...]e in the flow of
[...]etween the ocean
[...]re." Dr Woods

Dr Woods said there was an
urgent need to establish, before
the end of the decade, a network
of instruments to make ocean ob-
servations, in order to improve
predictions of positive feedback
processes.

"We don't have enough obser-
vations today to test the models.
We have to have a massive international push. It's the critical is-
sue in many ways."

■ Hosepipe bans, already in force
in parts of Kent, Humberside and
the Thames Valley, will be ex-
tended to other areas of Britain
this week as water levels in some
places fall to record lows.

Residents in South-east England, Yorkshire and the West
[...] are most likely to be

New risk from CO₂ revealed

By Robert Matthews
Science Correspondent

CARBON dioxide contributes far
more to the greenhouse effect than
previously thought, according to new
research to be discussed at a conference on climatic change which opens
tomorrow.

The research, by the independent
[...] Resource Defence Council in
[...] and submitted to
[...]plications for
[...]ing.

This increase in the importance
carbon dioxide stems from a reasse
ment of the importance of the ot
pollutants, methane and chloroflu
carbons (CFCs). Methane is us
taken to be 25-30 times more pot
greenhouse gas than carbon di
molecule for molecule. Howev
relatively short atmospheric l
of 10 years means its real po
3.5 times that of carbon dioxi

Dr Lashof said this does n
that sources of methane, suc
tle and leaks from gas pipe
ignored: "We should still w
[...], as there is a potenti
[...] very cost-effec
[...] life-time

...NG SPELLS MORE DISASTER AHEAD FOR OUR PLANET IN THE CHAOTIC NINETIES

[...]e winds of change

[...]o be
[...]nter
[...]han
[...]mer
[...]toco
[...] bas

[...]ing s
[...]or ea
[...]d call

Eye of the storm ... Gales could become a fact of life for Brit

in the
worse.
[...]getting
[...], there
[...]t years
[...]cords
[...]world
[...]elsius
[...]s in

increased by 25 per cent.
The rise in temperature
matches the increase in
carbon dioxide.

It is not just Britain that
has been affected. There
have been recurring
droughts in places like
Ethiopia and the Sud

a result of the Greenhouse
Effect. But added
together, the evidence is
overwhelming. The pat-
tern matched the predic-
tions of global warming
made by climatologists.

Fu[...]
Italy
dryi[...]
turni[...]
21st [...]

Lo[...]

Warmer world skates on even thinner ice

Climatology

Scientists from
Cambridge University
working at the North
Pole have discovered

per cent. Knowing the amount
below the water's surface, the
scientists were then able to calculate the precise thickness of
the ice sheet at any point.

A series of measurements was
taken along 30-mile stretches of
Arctic ice sheet on both

TOO HOT
TO HANDLE?
The Greenhouse Effect

Mary Gribbin with John Gribbin

Cartoon Illustrations by Jon Riley

CORGI BOOKS

TOO HOT TO HANDLE? THE GREENHOUSE EFFECT

A CORGI BOOK 0 552 542954

First publication in Great Britain

PRINTING HISTORY

Corgi edition published 1992

Text copyright © 1992 by Mary and John Gribbin
Cartoon illustrations © 1992 by Jon Riley
Technical illustrations © 1992 by Industrial Arts Studios

Cover photo © Tony Stone Worldwide

This book is set in 13/16 pt Bembo by
Chippendale Type Ltd., Otley, West Yorkshire.

Corgi Books are published by Transworld Publishers Ltd., 61–63 Uxbridge Road, Ealing, London W5 5SA, in Australia by Transworld Publishers (Australia) Pty. Ltd., 15–23 Helles Avenue, Moorebank, NSW 2170, and in New Zealand by Transworld Publishers (N.Z.) Ltd., Cnr. Moselle and Waipareira Avenues, Henderson, Auckland.

Made and printed in Great Britain by
Thomson Litho Ltd, East Kilbride, Scotland

Sources of material have been acknowledged where appropriate. The publishers would be pleased to rectify any errors or omissions in a subsequent reprint.

The newspaper headlines are used by permission, where possible: 'Warmer world skates on even thinner ice' is by Robin McKie, from and © *The Observer*, London, 22/7/90; 'The greenhouse time bomb' is from *The Independent*; 'UN warns of global timebomb' is from and © *The Guardian*; 'The winds of change' is from the *Daily Express*; 'New risk from CO_2 revealed' is from the *Sunday Correspondent*.

Too Hot to Handle? The Greenhouse Effect is printed on paper produced by Inveresk, Caldwells Mill, an environmentally friendly paper mill. The paper pulp is over 50% virgin woodpulp sourced from suppliers with a clear policy of reforestation and protection of wildlife. It is not chlorine-bleached so that cancer-causing dioxins are not produced. The mill does not use woodpulp from the rain forest areas, which is anyway of little use in paper making. All products from Caldwells Mill are 100% recyclable and biodegradable.

CONTENTS

CHAPTER ONE

Hothouse Earth

The world is hotter than it has ever been since scientists began to measure, and keep a record of, its temperature. The hottest year ever recorded was 1990. The six next hottest years ever measured worldwide all came during the 1980s, making it the hottest decade ever recorded. The two hottest years in the 1980s were 1988 and 1987. They were therefore the second and third hottest years since accurate temperature records began more than 150 years ago.

Even though the world has become warmer, the change in temperature during the twentieth century has really been quite slow. The world has slowly warmed up by about 0.5°C in the space of 100 years. But even this tiny increase in world temperature is a big change compared with natural shifts in global weather patterns. It means that even the coldest years in the 1980s were hotter than any year before 1920. And anybody who died before 1980 never lived through a year when the world was as hot as we experienced six times in the 1980s.

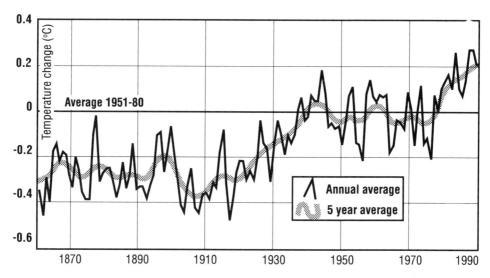

The average temperature of the Earth has been rising for more than 100 years. The temperatures shown here are the differences during the period 1861-1989 from the average for 1951-80 (Source: Climatic Research Unit, University of East Anglia)

A CHANGE IN THE WEATHER

While the world has been getting warmer, weather patterns have been changing in other ways as well. There is less rain than there used to be in a whole band of countries in the northern hemisphere, from the Caribbean across Africa to India and the Far East. All these countries lie near the equator, in what geographers call the 'subtropical latitudes'. Ethiopia, a country in Africa, has suffered terrible famines because there has not been enough rain to make the crops grow. At the same time, while there is less rain than there used to be in the subtropics, there is more rain falling each year further north, away from the equator, away from the sub-tropical latitudes. And the same pattern is happening in the southern hemisphere. Sub-tropics are getting less rain; higher latitudes, away from the equator, are getting more rain. There have been droughts in Africa, but there have been devastating floods in countries such as Bangladesh. Hurri-canes have got stronger, smashing a trail of destruction across countries in Central America and the West Indies, and even the United States. Even southern England felt the blast of hurricane-force winds in the great storm of 1987.

While all this has been going on, the sea level has been quietly creeping upwards. Scientists measure the height reached by the tides at many sites around the world, and

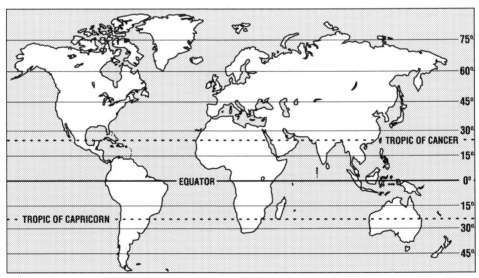

The world map

have done so for more than 100 years. When all these measurements are put together, they show that the height of the sea has been going up by about 1 centimetre every ten years over all that time. It doesn't sound much, but by the year 2000 the seas will be nearly 15 centimetres higher than when these measurements began. Because of this, the world's sandy beaches are disappearing, being washed away by the ever-rising tides.

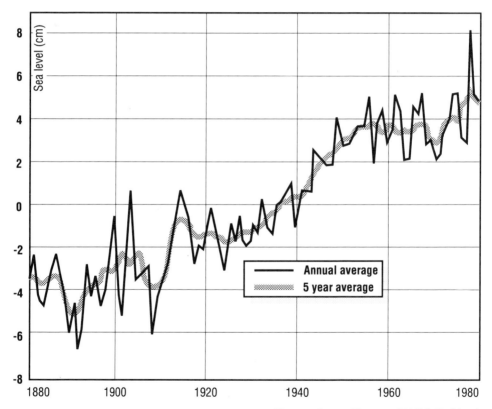

Sea levels have been rising (in relation to average levels) during the twentieth century

(Source: James Hansen, NASA Goddard Institute)

Vanishing beaches are bad news for people going on their summer holidays. There is also

bad news for people who like winter sports. The mountain glaciers in many parts of the world are melting, shrinking away like blocks of ice left out in the sun. At the end of the 1980s and the beginning of the 1990s, skiing resorts often had to close down for lack of snow.

Scientists believe that all these changes are a result of human activities. Gases that we are putting into the atmosphere around the Earth are trapping heat that should be escaping into space. This is making the Earth warmer and upsetting the climatic balance. Because a greenhouse also traps heat and stops it escaping, making it warmer inside the greenhouse than outside, this is known as the 'greenhouse effect', and the gases responsible are called 'greenhouse gases'.

The manmade greenhouse gases that are trapping heat in the atmosphere are carbon dioxide, the chlorofluoro-carbons (or CFCs) that also destroy the ozone layer, methane, and nitrous oxide. They are released from power station chimneys, from car exhausts, by industry and by agriculture, and more of these greenhouse gases are being released every year. So, the world will get even hotter as we move into the next century.

LESSONS FROM HISTORY

By the time somebody who is twelve years old today is

twenty-five years old, the world will be at least another 0.5°C warmer. That will make it one full degree warmer than it was at the beginning of the twentieth century. And we can see the importance of even such a small change in temperature by looking back to the time when the world was just 1°C colder than the average for the twentieth century. A time when great rivers in Europe, including the Thames, froze regularly in winter, crops failed, and people could not grow enough food to eat. Vegetables, fruit and the corn needed to make flour could not grow properly because frost killed the plants and it was too cold for seeds to germinate and grow into new plants. It was a time when the weather was so harsh that it has gone down in history as the 'Little Ice Age'.

This 'Little Ice Age' happened just a few hundred years ago and was at its worst in the seventeenth century, when William Shakespeare and Isaac Newton were alive.

Even though he was a scientist, Isaac Newton didn't leave us records of the weather when he was alive. But Shakespeare did. In his play, *Love's Labour's Lost*, he wrote about very cold winter weather:

When icicles hang by the wall,
And Dick, the shepherd, blows his
*   nail,*
And Tom bears logs into the
*   hall,*
And milk comes frozen home in
*   pail.*

This description suggests that winters in southern England

were colder in Shakespeare's day than they are now. Other evidence bears this out. References to the weather conditions of their time found in the work of poets, playwrights and storytellers are very useful because we have no direct records of temperatures from those days, before thermometers were invented. But as well as poetic images like Shakespeare's, there are written records of harvests, the time of the last frosts in spring and the first frosts in autumn. By studying all the information that was written down at the time about weather conditions and agriculture it is possible to work out what the weather at that time was really like. The best picture of the cold of the Little Ice Age comes from the records of when the River Thames froze hard at London.

THE FROZEN THAMES

In the first 1,000 years after Christ, there are mentions of the Thames being frozen at least eight times. This is no more than a rough guide, because the records from those days are incomplete. Reliable records begin in the twelfth century, after the Norman conquest of England. At first, there still seems to have been about one really hard winter each century.

Accurate records of when the Thames froze, and how hard it froze, begin with accounts of the winter of 1149–50, when the river froze so hard that men could cross on horseback at London. It

froze again in 1204–5. Then, in 1209, the famous London Bridge, mentioned in the nursery rhyme, was built.

This bridge was so solid that the gaps in its arches were narrower than the pillars that held the bridge up. It was half bridge, half dam. The water used to collect upstream from the bridge and pour through the arches in a waterfall, like a weir. As well as water piling up at the bridge, any rubbish floating in the water collected there too. Tree branches might get stuck, and if it was cold enough for ice to begin to form then the floating ice, like tiny icebergs, would pile up at the bridge, freezing to it and to any other rubbish caught there, and spreading an icy sheet outwards across the river.

So, after 1209, it was easier to make the river freeze solid than it had been before. But it still froze much more often in some centuries than in others, showing how the pattern of weather and climate changed as time went by.

In 1269–70 the Thames froze so far downstream that goods being taken to the City of London had to be sent overland from the Channel ports instead of going upriver by barge as they normally did. Between Christmas 1281 and March 1282 the ice on the frozen river was thick and strong enough for people to walk across. London Bridge itself was damaged by large lumps of ice both in that winter and during the winter of 1309–10.

The rest of the fourteenth century seems to have been milder, and for nearly the first 200 years after the bridge was built there were still only one or two winters each century when the river froze at London. But things began to change in the fifteenth century.

Between 1407–8 and 1564–5 the river froze a total of six times. Horses and carts were driven across the ice on several of these occasions, which must have annoyed the toll collectors on the bridge. Henry VIII is said to have driven a carriage on the river, either in the winter of 1536–7 or the following year, and his daughter, Elizabeth I, took a walk on the frozen ice covering the Thames in the winter of 1564–5. This was just after Shakespeare had been born, and there were many more hard winters coming for him to experience as he grew up.

In the seventeenth century, the frozen river became almost a regular winter sports arena.

A Frost Fair

(© Hulton Picture Company)

The first 'Frost Fair' that we know about was held on the Thames in 1607–8. Booths set up on the ice sold food, beer and wine, and there was bowling, shooting and dancing on the ice. Skating was introduced to Britain from the continent in 1662–3. We know this because the histories tell us that King Charles II watched the skaters enjoying their new sport on the frozen river during that winter. Altogether, there were ten winters cold enough to freeze the river in the seventeenth century, compared with just six between 1400 and 1600, and even fewer in the previous two centuries. We can see just how cold the Little Ice Age really was by looking at the greatest Frost Fair of all, held in 1683–4.

The ice was nearly 30 centimetres thick in places, and the river was completely frozen over for two months. So many shops and sideshows appeared on the ice that it was like another city, arranged in proper streets and including a printing press, whose owner made a small fortune by selling slips of paper printed with the customer's name and the slogan 'printed on the Thames'.

Even the king had his name printed at the printing shop on the ice.

R.D. Blackmore, the English novelist who lived in Victorian times, based the description of terrible winter weather in his famous novel, *Lorna Doone*, on the records of bad weather that actually occurred in the winter of 1683–4.

After the end of the seventeenth century, the world warmed up again slightly. There were another ten winters cold enough to freeze the Thames at London between 1700 and 1814, but there have been none since. London Bridge, which had been in the process of falling down for a long time (as the nursery rhyme tells us), was finally demolished in 1831, more than 600 years after it was built. By then, scientists at last had accurate thermometers to tell them what was happening to the weather.

The Little Ice Age that began in the sixteenth century, shortly before Shakespeare was born, had ended by about 1850. It had lasted roughly 300 years. When King Charles II had his name printed on a piece of paper on the frozen river in 1683–4, London Bridge was already more than 470 years old. But the time from that greatest of Frost Fairs to the present day is less than 320 years. We are closer in time to that great Frost Fair than Charles II was to the building of the bridge.

THE ICE AGE

All of these changes were caused by the world getting only about 1°C cooler. Nobody knows why this happened, but the world's weather does seem to change naturally by a degree or so on a timescale of centuries. The important point is that weather which people have been used to during the twentieth century, what we think of as 'normal' weather, is only 1°C warmer than a little Ice Age. Small changes in the average temperature of the world really do make a huge difference to weather patterns.

Geological evidence reveals

that the world's weather roughly falls into a pattern of 100,000 years of ice followed by 10–15,000 years of warmer weather called an 'interglacial'. We are in an interglacial at the moment. Nevertheless, before the 1980s the world was less than 4°C warmer than it had been during the great Ice Ages hundreds of thousands of years ago, when glaciers spread their icy fingers far down into Europe and North America.

We know how far the glaciers spread because they left their traces behind. Valleys were gouged out by the glaciers, rocks were scratched as they ground past, and heaps of rubble were dumped at the ends of the glaciers where the ice

A glacier

melted. We know when the great ice sheets covered the Earth, because traces of their passage are, in many places, buried beneath soil that has built up over the centuries, and scientists know how long it takes for the soil to become a certain thickness. We know how cold it was when the ice sheets covered the northern latitudes, partly because seeds and pollen were left behind by the ice, revealing what plants grew in which places; and because of changes in the molecules, the actual structure, of the ice itself.

By collecting together all the evidence, we now know that the most recent Ice Age was between 120,000 and 15,000 years ago when the world was a lot colder than it is today. There were also other Ice Ages, before 120,000 years ago, but this most recent Ice Age is the one we know most

about. Because of this, it is often called *the* Ice Age, even though we know there were other ones before it.

Greenland and Iceland lay gripped in a frozen sea during the latest Ice Age, and were completely covered by glaciers. A great ice sheet covered 6.6 million square kilometres of northern Europe, from Britain to the Baltic and into Russia. The greatest ice sheet of all

covered Canada and a large part of North America. The edge of the ice sheet ran from

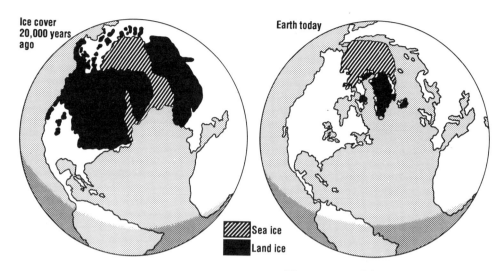

Ice cover
20,000 years
ago

Earth today

Sea ice
Land ice

The ice cover of the northern hemisphere during the latest Ice Age, compared with present-day ice cover
(Source: J. Imbrie and K.P. Imbrie)

Montana, in the Rocky Mountains, to New York, on the east coast of the United States. It covered an area of more than 13 million square kilometres – bigger than the Antarctic ice cap is today. And as well as these great ice sheets, mountain glaciers spread out from regions like the Alps in Europe, and the mountainous regions of South America and New Zealand, Tasmania, China and Japan.

GETTING HOTTER FAST

The worst weather of the most recent Ice Age, about 20,000 years ago, was only about 3.5°C colder than the average temperature during the twentieth century before 1980. The amount of warming up of the

Earth that brought an end to that Ice Age and made the world an easier place for people to live, was less than the difference between summer and winter in Europe or North America.

That temperature rise took place very quickly, by the standards of natural changes in climate. It took about 3,000 years for the world to warm completely out of the Ice Age. In round terms, the rate at which the world warmed up was 1°C every 1,000 years.

In the twentieth century, the world has already warmed by 0.5°C in less than 100 years. Scientists believe that this is due to the greenhouse effect of gases released by human activities – due to pollution of our atmosphere. If the warming carried on at the same rate, the world would be 3.5°C warmer in 700 years. Such a warming would be five times quicker

than the natural warming that ended the Ice Age. As far as we know, it would be quicker than any large natural climate change that has ever occurred.

But scientists who study the climate (climatologists) believe that the world will actually warm up much more quickly than that. Because we are putting more and more polluting gases into the air, the greenhouse effect is getting stronger and stronger each year. So much of these greenhouse gases is getting into the air now that the climatologists think the world will be 3.5°C warmer by about 2040. The same amount of change that occurred naturally over a span of 3,000 years will be happening in just fifty years – *sixty* times faster than any warming our planet has ever experienced!

That is why climatologists are worried about the greenhouse effect, and warn that it is important to take action *now* to slow down the release of greenhouse gases. If we do not, the world's climate may change so quickly that living things could not adapt fast enough. Forests would die, crops fail, and animals and people would not have enough food. When people do not have enough to eat, they are forced to move to other places, perhaps even other countries. This could make things difficult for the countries that do have food, and cause political upheavals or even wars. Animals that did not have enough food would die. Not just individual animals would be lost, but whole species that could not adapt fast enough to the changes.

CHAPTER TWO

The Heat Trap

The greenhouse effect is a kind of heat trap. It lets heat from the Sun in through the atmosphere to warm the surface of the Earth but it stops some of the heat that rises up from the surface of the Earth escaping into space. It can do this because the heat coming from the Sun is different to the heat coming from the ground.

Heat is a form of energy. The energy that comes to us from the Sun is mostly in the form of light waves. Light is a form of radiation, like radio waves but with much shorter wavelengths. The Sun radiates energy. Sunlight, which is short-wavelength radiation, passes through the atmosphere of our planet as easily as it passes through a pane of glass in a greenhouse.

How the heat trap works

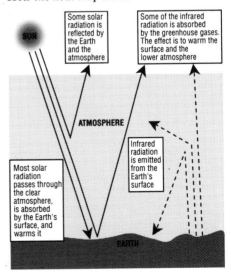

Some solar radiation is reflected by the Earth and the atmosphere

Some of the infrared radiation is absorbed by the greenhouse gases. The effect is to warm the surface and the lower atmosphere

ATMOSPHERE

Infrared radiation is emitted from the Earth's surface

Most solar radiation passes through the clear atmosphere, is absorbed by the Earth's surface, and warms it

EARTH

The energy from the Sun makes the Earth warm. The warm surface, the land and sea, houses, trees, grass and people, also radiate energy. This radiation has longer wavelengths, in between the wavelength of light and radio waves. It is called infrared radiation, or infrared heat.

INVISIBLE ENERGY

The colours of the spectrum (red, orange, yellow, green, blue, indigo and violet) correspond to different wavelengths of light. Red has the longest wavelength of these colours. Blue light has a shorter wavelength than red light, and violet light has the shortest wavelength of any of the colours of the spectrum. Infrared heat is like an invisible colour, with a wavelength longer than red light.

Although our eyes cannot see infrared 'light', some animals, such as snakes, can detect infrared heat and use it to see. Special video cameras can also see in the infrared, and use infrared 'light' to make pictures we can see. These are sometimes used to see in the dark, or by firemen searching for people in buildings full of smoke.

Although we cannot see infrared heat with our eyes, we can feel it on our skin. Infrared heat is the warmth we feel when we hold our hands near to a hot radiator but without touching it.

The energy radiated by the Earth is different from the energy radiated by the Sun because it has a longer wavelength. This is because the Earth is colder than the Sun. *Everything* radiates energy, even an ice cube. But the wavelength of the radiation is

longer if the temperature of the object is lower. It makes no difference what the object is made of. All that matters is its temperature.

The temperature of the surface of the Sun is about 6,000°C. Any object with such a high temperature radiates visible light, especially orange and yellow light. The temperature of the surface of the Earth is about 15°C, if you take an average over the whole planet. It gets all its heat, except for a tiny bit from volcanoes, from the Sun. Any object with that kind of temperature radiates infrared energy, *not* visible

light. But the Earth would be even colder if it were not for the greenhouse effect.

The Earth and the Moon are very nearly the same distance from the Sun. Each square metre of the Moon's surface gets the same amount of energy from the Sun as each square metre of the Earth. But the average temperature over the whole Moon is about *minus* 20°C. It is 35°C colder than the Earth. This is because the Moon has no atmosphere to trap heat.

On Earth, when infrared radiation from the ground tries to get out into space, some of it is trapped by molecules of carbon dioxide and water vapour in the air. This is a natural greenhouse effect. It makes our planet 35°C warmer than it would be if it had no atmosphere, and it makes the planet warm enough to provide a comfortable home for us. The *natural* greenhouse effect is a good thing, and without it we would not be here.

The natural greenhouse effect explains why it is warmer at sea level, where the heat is trapped, than it is on top of a high mountain, even though the mountain top is closer to the Sun.

THE GOLDILOCKS PLANET

We can see the value of our natural greenhouse effect by looking at the two planets nearest to the Earth – Venus and Mars. Unmanned space-probes have visited both these planets, so we know a lot about them.

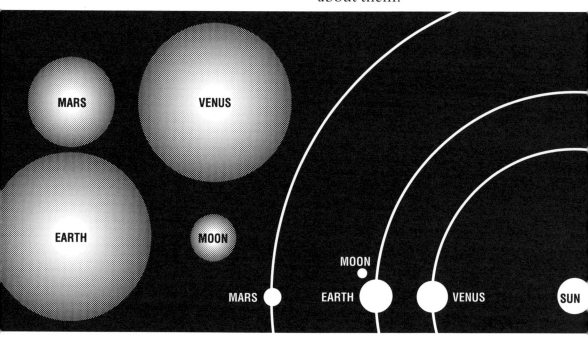

Planets and their relative sizes and positions in space

Venus is nearly the same size as the Earth, but it is a bit closer to the Sun. It has a very thick atmosphere with lots of carbon dioxide. The greenhouse effect on Venus is much stronger than it is on Earth. Because of this, the temperature at the surface of Venus is more than 500°C. This is much too hot for there to be any water on the planet, and we could not live there.

Mars is a bit further away from the Sun than Earth is. It is a smaller planet than either Venus or Earth, and although its atmosphere is mainly carbon dioxide, it is very thin – thinner than the air on top of a high mountain on Earth. Because the atmosphere is so thin, the greenhouse effect is very weak on Mars, and the temperature at the surface of the planet is always less than the freezing point of water. We could not live there either.

Astronomers sometimes call Earth 'the Goldilocks planet', because the temperature is like baby bear's porridge – just

right. It is just right because of the natural greenhouse effect. The problem today is that many of the things people do to make life more comfortable add extra greenhouse gases to the air. This is too much of a good thing, and it is making the world warmer.

CARBON DIOXIDE: THE MAIN CONTENDER

The main gas released by human activities is carbon

dioxide and excess carbon dioxide contributes directly to the problem of global warming.

Of course, like all animals we breathe out carbon dioxide; but this is not the problem. The carbon dioxide we breathe out is taken up by plants during the process called photosynthesis, and is broken up to release oxygen and to provide carbon to help make the tissues of the plant. The carbon just goes round and round the cycle, being absorbed by a plant that gets eaten, getting breathed out, and then being absorbed by another plant.

In the first place, the carbon dioxide came from volcanoes. Even though volcanoes are still active on Earth today, and still release carbon dioxide, they are

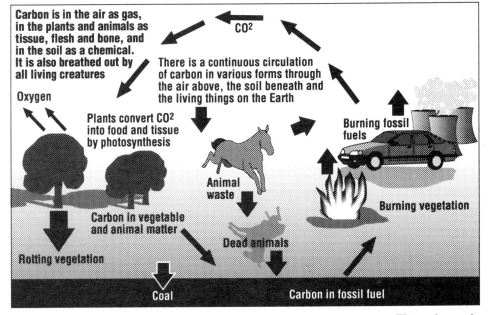

The carbon cycle

not in themselves the source of the problem. The amount of carbon dioxide in the air would not keep increasing naturally, for two reasons. First, some carbon dioxide is taken out of the air by chemical reactions and helps to form rocks such as limestone. Secondly, some of the carbon in living things gets trapped as the years go by, buried and taken out of circulation; it slowly builds up below ground. These natural processes keep the greenhouse effect in check.

However, extra carbon dioxide is made when we burn coal, oil or natural gas, which are known as fossil fuels. They are called fossil fuels because they are made from the remains of living things that died millions of years ago. Those remains got trapped underneath layers of mud that hardened and were turned into rock by geological forces,

while the remains themselves turned into fossil fuel. Whenever we burn fossil fuel, whether for industry, driving our cars or simply lighting and heating our homes, we release carbon that has been out of circulation for millions of years. This huge extra source of carbon dioxide greatly increases the ability of the atmosphere to trap heat.

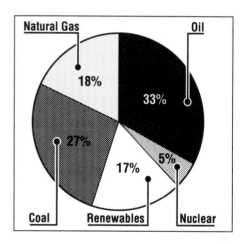

The proportions of different fuels around the world. Everything except nuclear power and 'renewables' (eg: wind, hydroelectric power) contributes directly to the greenhouse effect and global warming **(Source: British Petroleum, Worldwatch)**

31

If we burn wood from forests that are properly managed, we do not add to the burden of carbon dioxide in the air. New trees growing in the forests absorb as much carbon dioxide each year as we release when we burn the wood that has been chopped down. Properly managed forests are a renewable energy source. Other renewable energy sources are windmills or hydroelectric power stations.

However, the amount of carbon dioxide in the air does increase when living plants are destroyed and not replaced, as is happening in many parts of the world. When forests are cut down, an enormous number of living plants are killed. Trees and other forms of plant life, especially the tiny plankton that live in the surface of the sea, are like the lungs of our planet, except that they work like our lungs in reverse. They

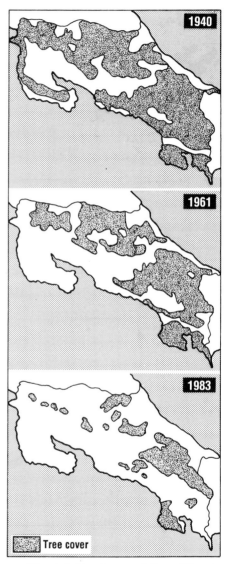

The shrinking forests of Costa Rica, in Central America

breathe in carbon dioxide and breathe out oxygen.

When plants die and decompose, or are burnt, the carbon they contain combines with oxygen to make more carbon dioxide – and those plants are no longer there to recycle the gas. So, again, carbon dioxide builds up in the air and the heat trap gets stronger.

Some people worry that if too many trees are cut down there will not be enough oxygen for us to breathe. This won't happen because there is so much oxygen in the air that even if all photosynthesis stopped tomorrow, we would be able to breathe for at least a million years without suffocating. If photosynthesis stopped tomorrow, though, we would have nothing to eat. And even if we did have a supply of food, long before we ran out of oxygen we would be in trouble because of the extra greenhouse effect.

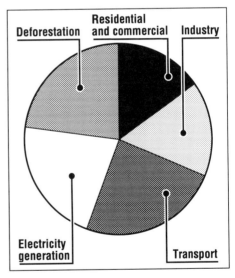

The contribution of different sources to man-made carbon dioxide emissions between 1980 and 1985 (Source: UK Department of the Environment)

TWO MORE INGREDIENTS

Human activities are also increasing the amount of methane and nitrous oxide in the air. Like carbon dioxide, these are both natural greenhouse gases, produced by living things. The amount of each gas is increasing mainly because of agriculture.

Nitrous oxide is also produced from the nitrogen fertilizers that are added to fields in large quantities today. It is sometimes known as 'laughing gas', because the effect of sniffing nitrous oxide is much the same as the effect of sipping alcohol. But nitrous oxide in the atmosphere is not so funny. Although the amount of the gas present in the air is very small, the concentration is likely to increase by a third, compared with its natural level, by 2030.

Methane is produced by single-celled organisms, bacteria, that live in swampy places. Methane produced from natural swamps is no problem because, like the carbon dioxide involved in photosynthesis, it gets recycled as part of the natural ecological balance of our planet. But rice paddies are like artificial swamps, and as more rice is grown to feed more hungry people around the world, the amount of methane in the air is increasing rapidly.

People are also responsible for producing methane when they bury their rubbish at landfill sites. The rubbish contains a lot of biological material – everything from waste paper to waste food – and bacteria quickly get to work on this, converting it into methane. 'Natural gas' that is used to heat our homes and cook our food contains methane, and

34

some of this (nobody is sure how much) escapes into the air each year from leaky pipelines. The gas is also often found by people drilling for oil, and since it is not as valuable as oil it may simply be allowed to escape into the air as an unwanted by-product.

Animals also produce methane. The stomach of a cow is a very good methane factory, and animals that chew the cud release a lot of methane when they belch. There are an enormous and increasing number of cows in the world because there is a demand for more and more meat for people to eat. This is not just because there are more people in the world each year, but because some countries have become richer. People like to eat meat and buy it if they can afford it, even though we can manage without it. In poorer countries, people eat almost

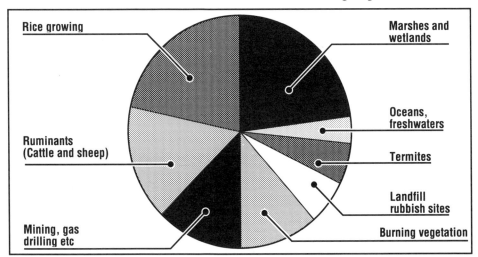

The contribution of different sources to the build-up of methane

(Source: UK Department of the Environment)

entirely vegetarian food; but when they get richer, they eat more meat.

Another natural source of methane also involves animals, but much smaller ones than cows. Termites release a lot of methane into the air from their bodies as they digest plant food. Each termite only releases a little methane, but a whole colony of termites produces a lot. However, nobody farms termites for food, and as far as we know this source of methane is not getting bigger.

There is, though, one big problem about 'natural' sources of methane.

As the world warms up, the frozen tundra of the far north, in places like Siberia and Alaska, will begin to thaw out and become more swampy. This will release more methane into the air. At the same time, the bacteria that make methane in natural swamps and in paddy fields will become more active as they warm up. So anything that makes the world warmer will automatically increase the amount of methane in the air. And, because methane is a greenhouse gas, that will make the world warmer still, which will release even more methane, and so on. This kind of process is known as a 'positive feedback', and it could make the world warm even more quickly as we move into the twenty-first century.

Methane feedbacks are particularly important, because a single molecule of methane can trap as much heat as twenty molecules of carbon dioxide. All things considered, it is no surprise that methane is sometimes referred to as 'the joker in the pack' by climatologists trying to work out how quickly the world is going to warm up.

BUBBLES IN THE ICE

We know how much of each gas is added to the air every year because concentrations are measured regularly at sites far away from any sources of pollution. One site is on the top of a mountain in Hawaii, in the middle of the Pacific Ocean. Another is at the South Pole. The amount of methane in the air increases by 1 per cent each year, and the amount of carbon dioxide in the air has increased by more than a quarter compared with the concentration before this kind of pollution started, as the Industrial

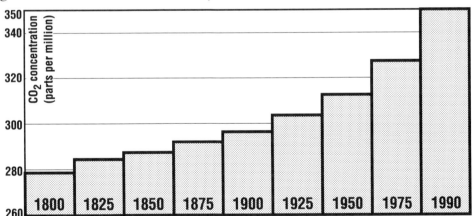

How the amount of carbon dioxide in the air has increased in recent years

(Source: US National Oceanic and Atmospheric Administration; measurements made at Mauna Loa, Hawaii)

Revolution became established about 150 years ago.

We can tell how much of each gas ought to be in the air because we can look back further into the past, to find out the composition of the air hundreds and even thousands of years ago. This is done by studying cores of ice drilled from the glaciers in Greenland and Antarctica.

When snow falls it is light and fluffy, and full of air. In these regions, the snow never melts. As more snow falls each year, it piles up and the buried snow gets squeezed and turned into solid ice. But the ice still has bubbles of air trapped in it.

Each year, a new layer of snow falls on the ice and is followed by more and more layers of snow. This would make the ice cap thicker, but old ice is squeezed out from the ice cap, like toothpaste out of a tube, to make glaciers.

Ice that formed from snow that fell hundreds of years ago, but hasn't yet been squeezed out, is buried deep beneath the surface. This old ice can be extracted from the ice cap using a drill like the ones used to drill for oil. The ice can be pulled out in a long core, and pieces of such cores can be kept frozen in laboratories around the world. There, scientists study the bubbles of ancient air in the ice.

They know the age of each layer of ice because they know how long it takes for a certain thickness of ice to build up. So they can suck out the air from bubbles 100 years old, or 1,000 years old, or any other age, down to the bottom of the ice core.

These measurements show that the amount of methane in the air was steady until about 200 years ago. Since then, it has doubled. The increase has occurred exactly at the time when the human population of our planet has increased rapidly.

A bigger population means that more food has to be grown to feed all the extra people, so there have been more rice paddies and more cattle in the world.

The amount of carbon dioxide in the air also stayed the same for thousands of years, until the nineteenth century. The increase since then exactly matches the destruction of forests and burning of fossil fuel that has gone on for the

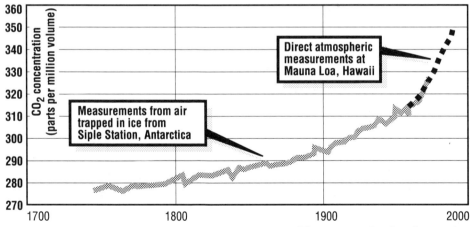

The ice cores also show how carbon dioxide started to build up in the air after the Industrial Revolution (Source: IPCC)

past 200 years. Today, about 2 billion tonnes of carbon that used to be stored in plants is turned into carbon dioxide each year, and more than 5 billion tonnes of carbon from fossil fuel is burnt each year. The amount of carbon dioxide in the air is increasing at a rate of 0.5 per cent every year.

CFCs: AN UNNATURAL INFLUENCE

And this is still not the end of the problem. As well as the increase in these natural greenhouse gases, human activities also release a completely 'unnatural' set of greenhouse gases into the air. These gases are known as chlorofluorocarbons, or CFCs. They have been in the news recently because they damage the ozone layer of the atmosphere, high above our heads, and cause the 'hole in the sky' that develops each spring over Antarctica.

The ozone layer is important because it shields us from the ultraviolet rays of the Sun. These can cause sunburn and even skin cancer and are bad for plants and animals, as well as for people. But this has nothing to do with the greenhouse effect. The 'hole' doesn't let in extra warmth to heat the surface of the ground. *As well* as making the ozone hole, and in a quite separate process, CFCs add to the greenhouse effect by trapping heat near the ground just as carbon dioxide or methane do. Indeed, molecule for molecule they are the strongest greenhouse gases. A single molecule of CFC can trap as much heat as 10,000 molecules of carbon dioxide.

There were no CFCs at all in the air before the 1930s, when they were invented by

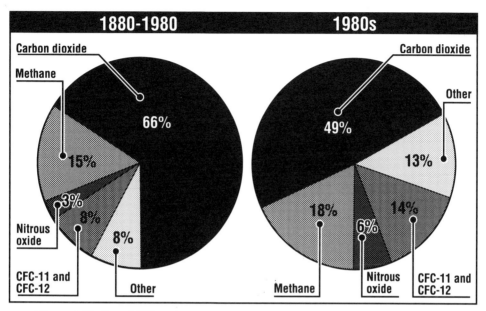

1880-1980

Carbon dioxide

Methane

66%

15%

3%

8%

8%

Nitrous oxide

CFC-11 and CFC-12

Other

1980s

Carbon dioxide

Other

49%

13%

18%

14%

6%

Methane

Nitrous oxide

CFC-11 and CFC-12

The contribution of different gases to global warming between 1880 and 1980, and during the 1980s. Other gases now make the problem more than twice as bad as the warming caused by carbon dioxide on its own

(Source: US Environmental Protection Agency)

industrial chemists. Since then, they have been used for many purposes. Some went into spray cans, to make the spray; some are used in refrigerators; and some are used to make the bubbles in foamed plastics. The two most common kinds are called CFC-11 and CFC-12,

but there are others as well. Of course, because people are worried about the damage to the ozone layer, chemists are now developing other gases to do the same work as CFCs. Some of these are known as HCFCs. Very often these new gases are also very good at trapping heat. 'Ozone friendly' doesn't necessarily mean 'environment friendly'.

Although there is not very much CFC in the air, its effectiveness at trapping heat still makes it the second biggest contributor to the extra greenhouse effect, after carbon dioxide. What's more, CFCs and HCFCs stay in the atmosphere for a long time once they are released. If we stopped making these gases tomorrow, there would still be some left in the air, trapping heat, in 100 years time. Methane and nitrous oxide together do not trap as much heat as the CFCs do.

There are many other gases which make a very tiny contribution to the greenhouse effect, but they are too many to list here and we don't need to worry much about any of them. The books listed under 'Further Reading' will help if you need more information.

Altogether, the extra green-house effect of all the other heat-trapping gases released each year now adds up to more than the contribution of all the carbon dioxide released by human activities each year. It is as if we were burning at least twice as much fossil fuel, and tearing down at least twice as much forest.

The greenhouse problem is therefore more than twice as bad as it would be if we only had to worry about carbon dioxide on its own. Scientists only began to realize in the 1980s how much heat is now being trapped by gases other than carbon dioxide, which explains why the greenhouse effect suddenly became a major cause for concern. When all of the heat-trapping gases are added together, and we allow for the fact that more and more of them are being released each year, the forecasts for the weather of the twenty-first century are alarming.

CHAPTER THREE

Future Weather

Climatologists use computer models to work out how the weather will change as the greenhouse effect gets stronger. These climate models are made out of numbers and equations stored in a computer. They calculate how the weather will change if some of the numbers in the model, such as the strength of the greenhouse effect, are changed.

Nobody can say for certain how hot the world will get in the next century. Computer models can tell how much extra greenhouse effect there will be *if* we carry on releasing more and more greenhouse gases each year. But if those forecasts are so frightening that governments and ordinary people burn less coal, ban CFCs, and don't release so much of the greenhouse gases, the forecasts will never 'come true'. That wouldn't mean that the computer models were wrong.

It's a bit like driving a fast car towards a bend. You know that if you don't slow down, you will crash. So you slow down and drive safely round the corner. Just because you got round the bend safely

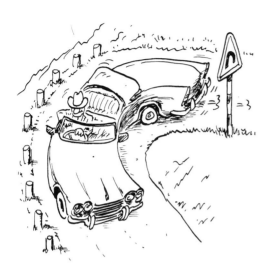

doesn't mean that the 'forecast' was wrong and there was no need to slow down!

The computer models tell us that the amount of greenhouse gases added to the air so far should make the world about 1°C warmer once it has had time to settle down to the change. But they also tell us that it takes a long time for the weather to become established in a new pattern, so only half of the warming should have happened yet.

EXTREMES OF ALL KINDS

The world has actually warmed by about 0.5°C during the twentieth century. If this is because of the greenhouse effect, the models tell us that there is still as much warming to come, even if we stop releasing more greenhouse gases. The delay is mainly because it takes a long time for the oceans to warm up.

There are other things that change the climate. For example, some people think that the Sun's heat has increased a little bit in the past 100 years. But measurements from satellites in space show that even if this has happened it is only enough to warm the world by 0.05°C – one tenth as much as the warming that has actually happened. Most climatologists agree that the extra greenhouse effect of gases put into the air by human activities is the main reason why the world is getting warmer.

Because we are still releasing greenhouse gases, by the time the world has caught up with this extra 0.5°C warming, there will be even more catching up to do as the greenhouse effect gets stronger.

The 1980s was the hottest decade since records began, so the weather of those years gives us a hint of what we can expect. But this is only a hint, because we can expect even more extreme weather in the next few decades.

In the late 1980s, tourists going on summer holidays to countries such as Greece and Spain found that it was too hot for comfort. Temperatures soared to 43°C. It was so hot that some people spent whole days sitting in their hotel swimming pools just to keep cool. Some people died because of the extreme heat.

In the middle of the United States, there were severe droughts in the summer of 1988. Crops failed on the great plains, where so much wheat is usually grown that it has been called 'the breadbasket of the world'.

But it was not just hot summers that made headlines. Ski resorts often had to close for

45

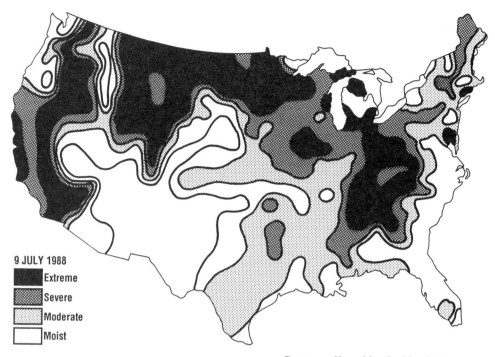

9 JULY 1988
- Extreme
- Severe
- Moderate
- Moist

Regions affected by the North American drought of 1988. Droughts like this will be more common as the world warms (Source: US Department of Agriculture)

lack of snow, and when they did get snow it was sometimes too much. Some very severe winter blizzards, fiercer hurricanes than ever before, and strong storms have struck Britain and Europe, especially in 1987 and 1990.

Experts say that this is just what you should expect as the world begins to warm up, because it does not warm up evenly. When the continent of Europe, for example, has a very mild winter, like the one of 1989–90, but the ocean

46

nearby is still relatively cold, very fierce winds blow to try to average out the difference between the temperature of the land and the temperature of the sea.

In the 1990s there will still be variations in the weather from year to year. It won't be hot and dry every summer. But the average temperature will be as high as the warmest years in the 1970s and 1980s. By the year 2000, temperatures will be a full 1°C higher than in 1980. By the decade of the 2010s, less than twenty years from now, even the cold years will be warmer than the warmest years of the 1950s and 1960s.

REGIONAL CHANGES

The computer models also tell us how different regions of the world will change as the average climate warms up. The great plains of North America, and all of southern Europe, will dry out. This is partly because the rainfall bands that 'belong' in those latitudes move north when the world warms. It is also because hotter summers will evaporate more moisture out of the soil.

Northern and western parts of Britain may get more rain, averaged over the whole year, because they are near the sea. When the world warms up, more water evaporates from the sea and falls as rain on nearby land. A lot of the rain will fall in winter. There will still be hot summers and droughts in Britain though, especially in the south-east.

Of course, it isn't just the northern hemisphere that will be affected, although since most people live north of the equator it is natural that attention often focuses on changes that will take place in the northern half of our planet. Australia, though, is among the countries that will be hardest hit by global warming. An Australian researcher, Graeme Pearman, estimates that by 2030 temperatures in Australia may be 3°C higher than in the 1980s, with 50 per cent more rainfall in summer but 20 per cent less rainfall in winter. Tropical storms that feed off warm water – cyclones – will occur further south than they do today as the ocean warms up, and may be hitting Brisbane regularly in the 2030s.

Apart from the problems this will cause in regions that are not used to such storms, when rain-bearing weather systems move south, Western Australia, in particular, may miss out entirely. Drought will be the problem there, disrupting agriculture. Similar problems will also severely reduce the flow from the Snowy River

complex of reservoirs and pipelines on the other side of the country, which today supplies most of the water required by the states of New South Wales and Victoria.

Only a very few regions of the world may actually benefit from the changes in climate between now and 2030. Mountainous New Zealand, for example, might benefit as sheep-grazing moves further up the hillsides and subtropical fruits can be grown further south. But this is very much an

exception. New Zealand has a very low human population and plenty of room in which agriculture can manoeuvre. More crowded regions, with less flexibility, would inevitably suffer badly. This is especially true in countries that depend on the monsoon rains for their crops. If the monsoon stops coming, there will be no food for millions of people.

Even so, it would be difficult, but not impossible, to adapt to a new pattern of climate. That has happened naturally in the past, when the weather changed naturally. At the end of the latest Ice Age, as we saw in Chapter One, the world warmed by about 3.5°C. The warming took about 3,000 years, and plants and animals had time to adapt. But things are different now. It is therefore time to look in more detail at the implications of the speed of the changes we can expect.

TOO FAST FOR COMFORT

Even without allowing for the 'extra' 0.5°C warming already built into the greenhouse effect, the world will be warming by about 0.5°C each ten years over the next few decades. This warming is hundreds of times faster than any natural climate change. In effect, this means that climate zones that 'belong' near the equator will move further north and south, to higher latitudes.

Even if the warming does not get any faster than 0.5°C every ten years, this corresponds to a shift in climate zones at a rate of 600 kilometres a century. Forests simply cannot move that fast.

When the world warmed at the end of the latest Ice Age, the fastest rate at which any forests spread northward was 200 kilometres a century. This

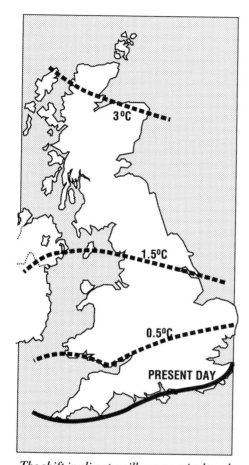

The shift in climate will move agricultural patterns northward in Britain. Maize (sweetcorn) could only just be grown in the south of England in most recent years (thick line), but could be grown in Yorkshire if the temperature rises by 1.5°C, and in Scotland if the temperature goes up by 3°C (Source: Martin Parry, University of Birmingham)

is the world speed-record for trees, and it is held by spruce. By the middle of the twenty-first century, trees like spruce, birch, maple, oak and beech will 'belong' as much as 500 kilometres north of where they live today.

The adult trees will probably survive for quite a long time in the 'wrong' places, but there will be no new saplings growing up to take their places. Where the weather will be right for the saplings, there will be no adult trees, and so there will be no seeds to grow into saplings.

Perhaps we can manage without trees, and all the things that depend on trees to survive. But how will farmers cope with such rapid changes?

Sometimes people think that the greenhouse effect might be a good thing for agriculture. In countries like Britain, a little warming might be helpful because it would mean fewer frosts. But if there are fewer frosts to damage the plants, there are fewer frosts to kill pests in winter. This means that farmers have to deal with worse attacks by pests and crop diseases after a mild winter.

In any case, we are not in for a *little* warming. We are due for a *big* warming – too much of a good thing. It is no help having crops survive the winter if they suffer drought in summer.

ONE PIECE OF GOOD NEWS

You might expect the extra carbon dioxide in the air to be good for plants, even if the temperature is a problem. After all, plants need carbon dioxide for the photosynthesis they use to grow.

Some plants do very well if they are given extra carbon dioxide, but others only benefit slightly. Crops that thrive with extra carbon dioxide, provided they also have enough water, include soya beans, wheat and barley. Maize or sweetcorn don't do so well. But some of the plants that flourish best are weeds, and these weeds may take over the land that farmers need to grow crops.

There are other problems. When some food plants are given extra carbon dioxide, each plant grows bigger. But

up more agricultural land. This means that farmers can still only grow as much food as they used to in the same field.

But there is one good thing about adding carbon dioxide to the air. It helps plants to manage with less water. Plants breathe in carbon dioxide through tiny holes in their leaves, called stomata. The same holes let out water vapour. When there is more carbon dioxide to breathe, the leaves grow with smaller stomata, or with fewer holes, because they do not need to take in so much air. This means that they lose less water. Extra carbon dioxide actually helps some plants to cope with drought. Unfortunately, this is only a small effect. It will not save plants from the kind of drought the great plains had in 1988.

Scientists have already measured the effect at work.

the plants grow so big that their leaves shade the leaves of the plant growing next to them. This stops the sunlight from getting through. So even if farmers manage to kill off the weeds, each plant they grow will be much bigger, and they will have to be planted further apart to give them enough light to grow properly. Bigger plants need more space and use

Leaves from different kinds of trees are collected by botanists and stored in collections known as herbaria. When researchers looked at old leaves, from 200 years ago, and compared them with fresh leaves from the same kinds of trees, they found that the modern leaves have fewer stomata, just as you would expect if they were getting more carbon dioxide with each 'breath' of air.

WHERE WILL IT END?

How far can the greenhouse effect go? Eventually, people will run out of things to burn, even if we do not come to our senses and stop burning coal and oil long before then. But there could be very big changes to come if we do not try to curb the greenhouse effect soon. Some of those changes can be guessed at by looking at what the world was like at different times in the past, when it was warmer than it is today. But there is one important difference. As long as we are still adding greenhouse gases to the air, the world cannot settle down in any of these natural warmer states. Nothing will be quite the same as it has ever been before, and living things will have no time to adjust to one new pattern of weather before it shifts into yet another pattern.

Climatologists measure such changes by comparing them with the average for the years from 1950 to 1979. The hottest weather since the Ice Age happened about 6,000 years ago when the average temperature of the world was 1.5°C higher than in the years from 1950 to 1979. Those are the kind of temperatures we will see again in the first decade of the twenty-first century.

So what was the weather like 6,000 years ago? Because the world was warmer, there was more evaporation from the oceans and more moisture in the air. The Sahara and the deserts of the Middle East were wetter than today, and there was more winter rain in the Mediterranean region.

This might mean more rain in places like Ethiopia where there have been terrible droughts recently. But even more rain would not solve Ethiopia's famine problems today, because so many people live in the regions on the edge of these deserts that farming has destroyed the soil. Where trees and grass used to cover the soil and hold it together, the land has been ploughed up, and the soil has blown away in the wind during the droughts. Deserts have spread not just because of drought but because of human interference with nature. Even if more rain does come to these regions for a time, a lot of the extra water will simply run away, eroding the soil even more as it does so.

But whether or not the extra rain does turn up and do any good in ten or fifteen years time, that weather pattern will have no time to settle down before things change again, and definitely for the worse.

Within thirty years, at the rate we are going now, the world will be warmer than it has been at any time since the Ice Age. About 125,000 years ago, before the latest Ice Age, the world was about 3°C

warmer than in the middle of the twentieth century. At that time, hippopotamuses, forest elephants and lions lived in the region where the River Thames runs through London today. That is probably the best picture of the kind of climate shift that will be happening in less than thirty years.

Changes will happen at sea as well as on land. As the world gets warmer, sea level rises because the water in the oceans expands. There is also more water in the oceans because glaciers and snowfields on the continents melt away.

So, just how high will the seas rise in our lifetimes?

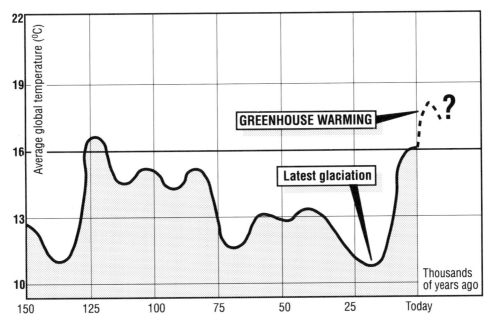

If we do not slow down the release of greenhouse gases, the world will warm faster than ever before in the next few decades, and it will soon be hotter than it has been for 125,000 years
(Source: James Hansen)

CHAPTER FOUR

Rising Seas

Half the population of the world lives in coastal regions. This is because these areas are good places to live. There is fertile soil, washed down from the mountains, rivers to provide fresh water and a route for transport, and the sea itself for shipping. The world population is increasing, so there is already a lot of pressure on coastal regions.

We know that sea level is rising. Over the past 100 years it has risen, on average, by a little more than 1 centimetre every decade. This is mainly because the water expands when it gets hotter. As the greenhouse effect speeds up over the coming years, experts calculate that sea level will rise by 10 centimetres every decade, and by more than 30 centimetres in total by 2030. Sea level will rise faster partly because the world is warming up more rapidly, and partly because snow and ice on mountains will be melting and adding to the amount of water in the sea.

A rise in sea level of 30 centimetres does not sound a lot. But in some parts of the world, this could be catastrophic.

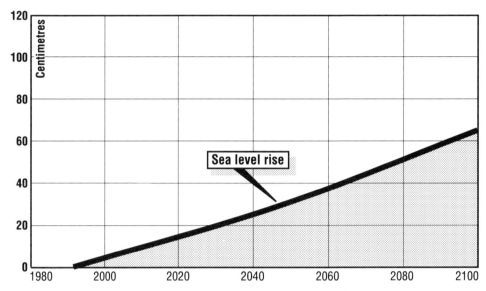

The rise in sea level that we can expect if we do not slow the emissions of greenhouse gases
(Source: IPCC)

Altogether, 3 billion people live in low-lying coastal regions, and this includes major cities such as London, Venice, Miami, Shanghai, Leningrad, Rio de Janeiro and Alexandria. In regions where there are great river deltas, such as the Nile and Ganges, millions of people are already vulnerable to flooding.

A rise in sea level of 50 centimetres would flood only 0.4 per cent of the area of Egypt. But 16 per cent of the country's population live on that land. An area of 1,754 square kilometres of cropland would be inundated and about 3.3 million people left homeless – even without allowing for any increase in population by the middle of

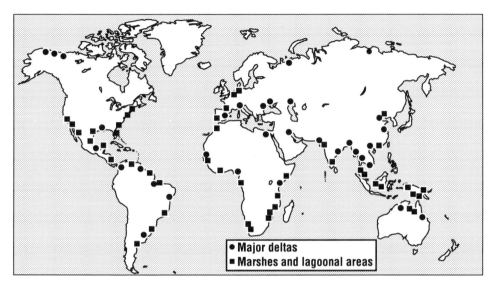

Regions of the world that are at risk from rising sea level (Source: US Environmental Protection Agency)

the twenty-first century.

Sea levels may have risen by a full metre by the end of the twenty-first century. That would remove 12 per cent of the land area of Bangladesh, make 9 per cent of its population homeless, and make 11 per cent of its agricultural land unsuitable for growing food.

THE HURRICANE CONNECTION

This is not the end of the problem. As the world begins to warm up, climatologists expect storms to become more common and more severe. This is partly because the world does not warm up evenly. Some places get hotter more quickly, and strong winds blow between the hot and cold regions, trying to average out the temperature. But that is not the only effect.

Very strong storms, such as hurricanes, actually feed off warm water. Water evaporates from the warm ocean and the vapour rises into the air. There, it condenses back into liquid water and falls as rain. When the vapour turns back into liquid it gives out just as much heat to the air as it took to evaporate the water in the first place. This heat is the energy that drives the winds of a hurricane.

In the past few years, hurricanes have occurred which are stronger than any observed before. This is an early sign of the growing greenhouse effect.

If a country such as Bangladesh is struck by extra-strong hurricanes and the sea level has gone up by 30 centimetres, the flooding will be even worse than if the sea level had gone up but the storms were the same srength as they used to be. Stronger winds will blow the floodwaters further inland. At the same time, fierce storms lift the water up higher.

Storms are low-pressure systems. This means that the pressure of air in a storm is low. When you suck a drink through a straw, the liquid rises up the straw because, by sucking, you create low pressure above the liquid. A great

storm sucks the water underneath it upwards even more strongly, like a giant vacuum cleaner. This raises sea level even more – sometimes by several metres – and makes the flooding even worse.

It is not only countries like Egypt and Bangladesh that will be affected. The Dutch spent the equivalent of $2.5 billion on a massive sea defence scheme to protect them from storm surges in the North Sea. The new barrier, which was completed in the 1980s, was designed to protect them from the kind of storm that ought to occur once in every 10,000 years. If sea level goes up by 1 metre, even without allowing for storms getting stronger, surges strong enough to overwhelm the barrier can be expected once every 100 years. In other words, the odds against the barrier being breached in any year are only

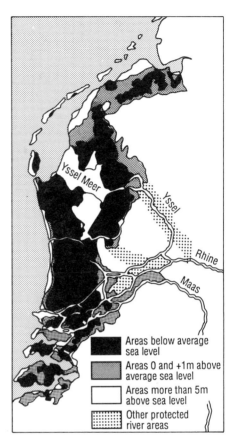

The region of the Netherlands at risk from rising sea level
(Source: UNEP)

100 to 1. It is more likely than not that it will be overwhelmed before the end of the twenty-first century.

The odds against the Thames Barrier surviving are just as bad. It is officially estimated that if sea level goes up at the expected rate, there is a fifty-fifty chance that the Thames Barrier will be broken through before the year 2050.

THE COST OF PROTECTION

Rising seas can be held back by building bigger and better sea defences, and people and industries can be moved inland, but both options are expensive. Improving the coastal defences of Great Britain to counter the rise in sea level expected over the next sixty years would cost about £10 billion.

A study carried out by the US Environmental Protection Agency calculated that a rise in sea level of 64 centimetres would cost the city of Charles-

Regions of Britain at risk from rising sea level over the next 100 years (Source: Institute of Terrestrial Economy)

ton, in South Carolina, just over $1 billion – the cost to just one city. The same rise in sea level would cost the city of Galveston, in Texas, $360 million.

Many countries at risk from rising sea levels, such as Indonesia and Thailand, have no way of raising the funds to provide equivalent protection. Indonesia has thousands of kilometres of coastline vulnerable to flooding and, because of rapidly increasing population, more and more people are moving into these areas. In Thailand, canals that were dug to bring fresh water to rice fields are already becoming tainted with salt water when storm surges occur – surges that may, of course, be being stimulated by, among other things, the greenhouse effect of the methane put into the air by those very rice fields.

Some people, however, could not hold back the sea at any cost. The Maldive Islands, in the Pacific, rise less than 3 metres above sea level today. The 177,000 people who live there have no hope of protect-ing themselves from rising sea level combined with increased storminess. By the year 2050, severe hurricanes may sweep the waves right over these islands, and similar low-lying countries.

Even where the waves are not so destructive, rising sea level is changing the world. Each 10 centimetre rise in sea level pushes the boundary between salt water and fresh water at the mouths of rivers 1 kilometre inland, and pushes more salt water into under-ground deposits of fresh water. This means that near coastal regions there is less fresh water for agriculture and for people to drink as the seas rise.

VANISHING BEACHES

But the most dramatic sign of rising sea level is the disappear-ance of the world's sandy beaches. At the beginning of the 1980s, before the link between the greenhouse effect and rising sea level was properly established, geographers were surprised to discover that more than 70 per cent of the total length of sandy coastline around the world has shrunk at a rate of at least 10 centimetres per year during most of the

twentieth century. Less than 10 per cent of the world's sandy coast is growing, and the remaining 20 per cent has stayed much the same.

The discovery was the result of a survey carried out by the International Geographical Union. It came about because a group of researchers who met at a conference in 1972 to discuss changes in coastlines around the world realized that although they all knew of many sandy beaches that were eroding, scarcely any of them knew any regions where sandy beaches were getting wider.

At that time, nobody was worried about the greenhouse effect, and nobody realized that sea levels were rising and beaches were crumbling. A group was set up to study the situation around the world. It involved 129 researchers, representing all countries that have a sea coast. They used old maps and charts, written descriptions of how the coast looked in the past, and modern air and ground photographs. They worked out how every major sandy beach in the world has changed during recent decades.

Many beaches were built up after the latest Ice Age ended, and over the thousands of years since then at any time some beaches have been growing and others shrinking. But recently there has been a change in the pattern, with more general shrinking of sandy beaches. Both the rise in sea level and the increased storminess of recent decades are contributing to this erosion.

The problem is made even worse because the land behind the beaches is often built up. If sea level rose in the past (for example, when the great ice sheets melted) then new beaches would be carved out further inland, and sand would build up on some of them. But now people have built sea walls to hold back the waves, and there are roads, houses and factories behind those sea defences. When the sea rises it washes away the old beach but cannot push inland to make a new one.

The problem is worst along the Atlantic coast of the United States. Many towns grew up there alongside ocean beaches. Very often the word 'beach' is still part of the town's name – even though the beach itself has vanished. Miami Beach in Florida is a good example. There, however, when the beach washed away, the city built a new one with sand sucked up from the sea floor.

The city's inhabitants thought it worth the cost in order to keep tourists coming in. If rising sea levels destroy the beaches, even if no damage is done to homes and farmland, the tourists will stop coming to many seaside towns, and people who live there will have no work to do.

While sea level is rising, geological effects mean that long stretches of the US Atlantic coastline are actually sinking, making the problem worse. The state of Massachusetts is losing 26 hectares of land each year to the sea – but Louisiana is losing 40 hectares each day, more than 15,000 hectares

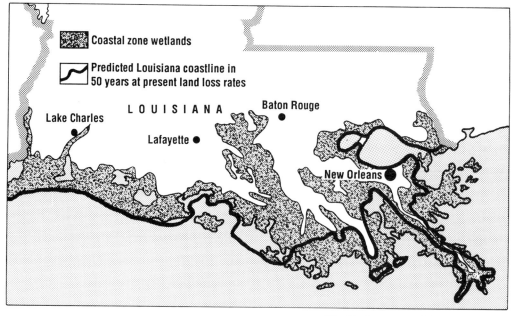

The likely retreat of the Louisiana shoreline by 2030 (Source: US Environmental Protection Agency)

(100 square kilometres) each year.

The same problem crops up all over the world. In Australia, a single stretch of beach in Sydney, 5 kilometres long, is all that stands between the sea and property worth £100 million. Singapore and the 'new lands' reclaimed from the sea nearby would be inundated by a rise in sea level of just over 20 centimetres.

GOODBYE TO THE BARRIER REEF?

Australia's Great Barrier Reef, one of the most remarkable natural structures on Earth, is also at risk from the rising seas. Living coral needs sunlight to grow, so it can only grow in shallow water. If sea level rises slowly, the living coral of the reef can grow upwards to compensate, so that the reef survives. But although delicately branching coral can stretch fingerlike branches upward at a rate of as much as 16 millimetres per year, the dense masses of coral that make the main structure of the reef grow at a maximum of 8 millimetres per year. That is just 8 centimetres per decade – and some estimates of the rate at which sea level will rise over the next fifty years are as high as 10 centimetres per decade. If that happens, the layer of water above the coral will get thicker. This will block out more sunlight and the coral will die.

That isn't the only problem. Parts of the reef are likely to be damaged and eroded by the increasing storm activity in a warmer world. And there is a limit to how much warmth coral can tolerate. The northern part of the reef, where water temperatures already climb above 30°C in summer, will be damaged and weakened when temperatures climb higher still, making the living coral more vulnerable to other problems, such as pollution, and reducing its ability to grow rapidly.

Even so, the picture of rising sea level is not as black as it is sometimes painted. Some people worry that sea level might rise much more quickly and to much higher levels.

The Great Barrier Reef   *(© Walter Deas / Planet Earth)*

That would happen, they say, if the great frozen ice sheets at the North and South Poles melted. But this is not something we should lose much sleep over.

IT COULD BE WORSE

First of all, the ice floating in the sea over the North Pole is not a problem at all, as far as sea level is concerned. Floating ice displaces the same amount of water that it would provide if it melted. You can see this if you put some water and some ice cubes in a glass and mark the level of the water. After the ice cubes have melted, the level is still the same. So, all the ice floating over the North Pole could melt without changing sea level.

As far as flooding is concerned, the ice we have to worry about is the ice on land,

especially the Greenland ice sheet and the Antarctic ice cap. Between them, Greenland and Antarctica contain more than 99.5 per cent of all the land ice on our planet today. Melting all the glaciers and snowfields, apart from those of Greenland and Antarctica, would raise sea level worldwide by just 33 centimetres. But this will not happen until the world has warmed by about 7°C.

Melting all the Greenland ice would raise sea level by 8 metres. Melting the ice of West Antarctica would produce a rise of 5 metres, and melting all of the ice in East Antarctica would increase sea level by 55 metres – but it is *not* going to happen in your lifetime.

The first thing that happens when the world begins to warm up is that these great ice sheets get thicker. The reason is simple. In a warmer world, more water evaporates from the oceans, so there is more moisture in the air. As long as the high latitudes, near the poles, are still cold enough, the extra moisture falls as snow over the ice caps.

The increase in thickness of the Greenland ice sheet has now been measured, using radar from satellites. It thickened by 23 centimetres each year between the late 1970s and the late 1980s. This is actually helping to slow down the rise in sea level. The extra water taken out of circulation and locked up in the Greenland ice each year corresponds to a change in sea level of 0.3 millimetres around the world.

The Antarctic ice sheet should be growing thicker more slowly, only one tenth as fast, because most of the ice is much further from the sea and gets less snowfall than the Greenland ice. Standard radar techniques cannot measure

such small changes, but researchers hope to measure the thickening of ice in Antarctica soon, using lasers mounted on satellites.

Some researchers estimate that a rise in temperature of 3.5°C would increase the amount of ice which is locked away in Antarctica each year by about 100 cubic kilometres. Even if more ice melts away from the edges of the great ice sheets in Antarctica and Greenland, and there are more icebergs breaking off and floating out to sea, the effect on sea level will still be roughly balanced by the extra accumulation of snow and new ice in the hearts of the ice sheets. On balance, the contribution of the great ice sheets over the North and South Poles to rising sea level over the next 100 years is likely to be nothing at all.

Eventually, if the temperature rises by more than 10°C

and stays there, all the ice sheets will melt. But ice melts very slowly, and 'eventually' means at least several hundred years. Either we will bring the greenhouse effect under control long before that happens, or we will have plenty of other problems to worry about as the climate changes dramatically.

So, how *can* we bring things under control?

CHAPTER FIVE

Helping Nature

People are not going to stop putting greenhouse gases into the air. We cannot imagine our world without fuel being burnt to provide energy and without intensive agriculture to feed a growing population. The problem is that burning fossil fuel creates carbon dioxide and intensive agriculture creates methane, and both these gases contribute to the greenhouse effect.

People in poorer parts of the world want to improve their standard of living with better housing and food, and things like refrigerators and TVs

which people in the richer parts of the world have become used to. Even more energy will be needed to meet their wishes, so the greenhouse effect will get stronger as we move into the twenty-first century, and the world will get warmer.

But there is a lot we can do to slow down the rise in temperature and shift of climate zones. This will make it much easier to cope with the changes. If the world warms by 3°C by 2030, it will be very difficult to cope with the speed of the change. If the warming is only 1°C by 2030, we will have time to adapt. Anything we can do to slow down the growth of the greenhouse effect is a good idea.

THE LUNGS OF THE PLANET

One of the best ways to help Nature to cope with the build-up of greenhouse gases is to stop cutting down forests, and to plant more trees. Trees take carbon dioxide out of the air while they are growing, and this gives a breathing space for people to find other ways to solve the greenhouse problem. Forests are sometimes called the lungs of the planet, although in fact they work the opposite way to your lungs, which breathe in oxygen and breathe out carbon dioxide. While it is growing, a tree takes in carbon dioxide and uses the carbon in it to build its trunk and branches. It doesn't matter where the trees are planted although, of course, they should always be appropriate trees for the region where they are grown.

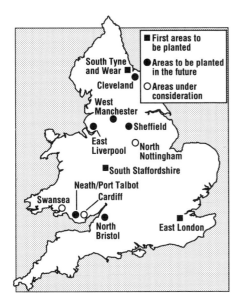

Plans for new community forests in England and Wales will help (a little bit!) to slow down the build-up of carbon dioxide in the air (Source: The Forestry Commission)

But just planting trees is not enough to solve the problem. We would need a new forest as big as the country of Zaire to take just one quarter of the carbon dioxide put into the air by burning fossil fuel each year. When the trees had grown up, you would still have to find a way to get rid of all the carbon locked up in their trunks without burning it.

To people in Europe or North America, it might look as if it would be easier just to stop destroying the rainforest in places like Brazil. If we leave the forest alone, we benefit because no extra carbon dioxide is put into the air and there are more living trees to absorb carbon dioxide. But the people who cut down these forests today have more urgent problems to worry about than the greenhouse effect.

GREENHOUSE ECONOMICS

A farmer who cuts down the trees to clear land for food-growing might see his family starve if the trees were preserved to slow the growth of the greenhouse effect. And there is another problem.

Many of the countries where the forests grow have been lent huge amounts of money by the richer countries to help them develop better industries and agriculture. The development plans have not always worked, but the debtor countries still have to pay back an enormous amount of money, as well as large interest charges on the loans. This means that they have to repay even more money than they originally borrowed.

This is good for the economies of the richer countries. It helps them to stay rich. But it means that other countries often have to cut down forests to provide land to grow crops that they can sell for cash, to raise the money to pay back the money they have borrowed. Meat for North American hamburgers often comes from cattle raised in South America on land that used to be forest.

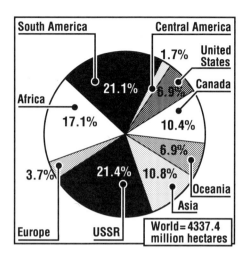

The distribution of the world's forests

In effect, rich countries are eating the rainforest.

If rich countries are worried about the greenhouse effect, one way they can help Nature is to cancel out some of these debts. Some people have suggested 'debt for nature' schemes, in which a country might guarantee to preserve its forests if an outstanding loan is cancelled.

Countries where rainforest is being destroyed today also have an embarrassing question

The very activities that made the rich countries rich have created the greenhouse problem. All the more reason why they should pay to help other countries improve their standard of living without letting global warming grow further out of control.

to ask of countries in places like Europe, North America and New Zealand. Where, they ask, have *your* forests gone? The truth is that most of the rich countries of the world used to be covered in forest as well, and most of the trees were cut down during the nineteenth century to provide fuel for industry and to open up new farmland. Countries like Brazil and Papua New Guinea are only doing today what our ancestors did not so long ago. And they are doing it for the same reason – to try to improve their lives.

SAVE ENERGY TO SAVE THE PLANET

Another way for the richer countries to help is by using less energy. If they could actually reduce the amount of fuel they burn each year, countries with a less luxurious standard of living could increase their energy consumption without worsening the greenhouse effect.

It would be very easy for Europeans and North Americans to use less energy, because so much of the fuel we burn now is wasted. Most of us just have not been used to making sure that our houses, including older ones, are insulated and have double glazing, for example, or that our cars and lorries use fuel as efficiently as possible. New buildings should be designed with energy conservation as a top priority. Many houses in Scandinavia are very good at holding heat in, so they need less fuel to keep them warm in winter, even though temperatures outside are low. If all the other countries of Europe built all new houses to the highest standards of insulation, they would save a lot of energy. And there are even simpler ways to cut down on energy use.

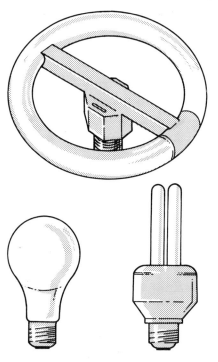

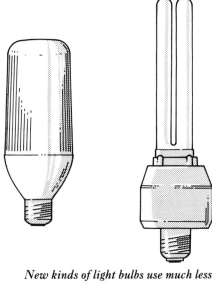

New kinds of light bulbs use much less electricity than the old kind but give just as much light. They save energy and help to slow global warming
(Source: World Resources Institute)

You can buy fluorescent light bulbs now that use only a fraction as much electricity but give just as much light as ordinary bulbs. Although the fluorescent bulbs are expensive to buy, they last longer than ordinary bulbs. Over the life of a bulb, it saves you as much money as the bulb costs, by using less electricity. If every house in Britain changed just two of its light bulbs to the new kind, that would save at least as much energy each year as the output of a large power station.

We can all save energy by turning lights off when we do not need them, turning central heating down a bit and wearing warmer clothes, and using cars less. If you have to use a car to get to school or work, try to arrange to share a car with your friends, instead of using several cars to make the same journey.

Because it takes energy to make anything we use, from a TV set to clothes or the food we eat, we can save energy by using less of everything and recycling as much as possible. Don't buy a new stereo, or bike or whatever just because it is this year's model, if last year's still works OK. Take your waste paper, cans and bottles to recycling dumps. In some places, you can even take an old fridge to a special dump, where the CFCs in its pipes will be taken out, returned to the manufacturer and used again, instead of being left to escape into the air and added to the greenhouse effect. Use kitchen and garden refuse to make a compost heap, and grow some of your own food if possible. When shopping, buy seasonal, locally-grown produce instead of exotic vegetables flown in from the other side of the world.

GOVERNMENTS MUST ACT

But individual people can only do so much on their own. Governments and industry must also do their bit. In a country like Britain, road vehicles produce more than a fifth of all the carbon dioxide released into the air each year. Cars should be designed to give more miles for each litre of fuel used. Reducing the speed limit on main roads would be one way of saving fuel, because cars use petrol more efficiently if they are driven more slowly. But in any case, cars should not be used more than absolutely necessary. One way to reduce car dependency would be to have large taxes on petrol, making it more expensive to use a car. The extra money from those taxes could be used to improve public transport so that people can use buses and trains instead of cars. And, of course, both

VINTAGE TRANSPORT MUSEUM

FAST CAR, c. 1992

cycling and walking are pollution-free means of travel!

Some countries already have laws which say that a machine like a refrigerator or a dishwasher must have a label telling you how efficiently it uses energy. This lets the person buying a new machine decide which one is more friendly to the environment. But advertisements for cars usually tell you how fast they can go, not how little petrol they use. If car manufacturers could be persuaded by governments to boast about fuel efficiency instead of speed, we could lessen the greenhouse threat *and* make the roads safer.

When will governments take this kind of action? Just as soon as enough people let them know they really care about the environment. Politicians like to get elected. If enough voters say they really want something done about the greenhouse effect, something will be done. So it really does help to write to politicians, get petitions organized, and let everybody know that you do care. Even if you are too young to vote now, let them know what policies you want to be able to vote for when you are old enough to do so!

The World Bank showed just how much could be achieved by looking at how energy could be saved in Brazil. The study showed that by spending $10 billion on more efficient vehicles, changing street lighting to fluorescent bulbs, and making domestic equipment like refrigerators more efficient, Brazil would reduce its energy needs drastically, slowing the build-up of greenhouse gases. And because less energy would be needed, and therefore less fuel burnt, the country would actually save money – $44 billion

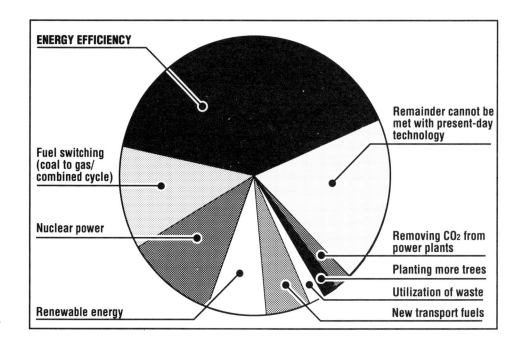

ENERGY EFFICIENCY

Remainder cannot be met with present-day technology

Fuel switching (coal to gas/ combined cycle)

Nuclear power

Removing CO2 from power plants

Planting more trees

Utilization of waste

Renewable energy

New transport fuels

How the United Kingdom might cut its emissions of carbon dioxide in half by 2020. Saving energy can do nearly half the job on its own, but there will also have to be new inventions (like the more efficient light bulbs that already exist) to help cut emissions by this much (Source: Energy Technology Support Unit)

according to the World Bank study, more than four times the cost of the scheme. The problem is, Brazil does not have a spare $10 billion to invest in energy-saving. Once again, the richer countries will have to help if these savings are to be made.

One way to provide energy

without releasing carbon dioxide into the air is by using nuclear power. Unfortunately, nuclear power on its own cannot solve the greenhouse problem. Many people are just as worried about building more nuclear power plants as they are about the greenhouse effect. They are frightened of radiation leaks, or accidents like the one at Chernobyl in the Soviet Union. But even without considering these problems, nuclear power can only help a little with the greenhouse effect.

NUCLEAR POWER ISN'T ENOUGH

France gets 70 per cent of its electricity from nuclear power, and that certainly means that less carbon dioxide goes into the air each year than if all those power stations ran on coal or oil. But in order to replace all the existing coal-fired power stations in the world with nuclear ones, and to cope with increasing energy demand, we would have to build more than 5,000 new nuclear plants by 2025. We would have to open a new nuclear power station every two and a half days for thirty-five years.

Building a power plant, of any kind, also 'costs' a lot in terms of carbon dioxide. All the building work, all the vehicles bringing material to the site and working on it, all the steel manufactured to use in the construction, and so on, take energy, which means carbon dioxide going into the air. It takes years for a new nuclear power plant to save as much carbon dioxide as was made during the construction of the plant.

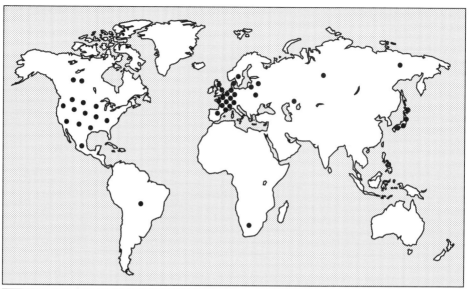

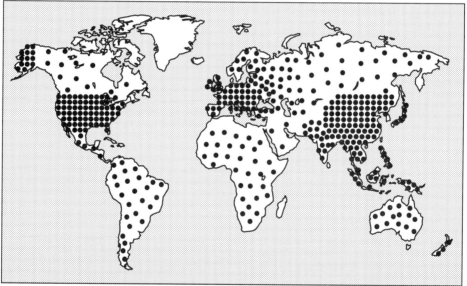

Each dot on these maps represents ten nuclear power stations. The top map shows those already built. The rash of measles over the bottom map represents 5,346 new nuclear power stations that we would need by 2025 if we make no effort to save energy, and shows where they would have to be built. This would still keep the amount of fossil fuel being burnt each year the same as in 1990. Saving energy is a much better way to reduce global warming than building nuclear power stations (Source: Greenpeace)

ENERGY EFFICIENCY IS BEST

We can do much better, in terms of the greenhouse effect, by spending the same amount of money on better insulation for homes, more efficient light bulbs, and so on. One study carried out in the United States showed that the cost of each kilowatt of 'new' nuclear electricity is seven times greater than the cost of *saving* a kilowatt of energy.

In some cities of the United States, power companies are now required by law to provide energy as cheaply as possible. They have found that when demand for electricity increases, instead of building a

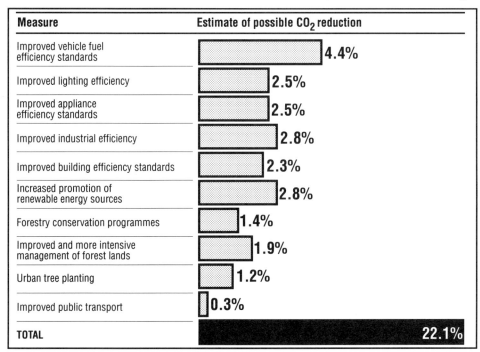

Measure	Estimate of possible CO_2 reduction
Improved vehicle fuel efficiency standards	4.4%
Improved lighting efficiency	2.5%
Improved appliance efficiency standards	2.5%
Improved industrial efficiency	2.8%
Improved building efficiency standards	2.3%
Increased promotion of renewable energy sources	2.8%
Forestry conservation programmes	1.4%
Improved and more intensive management of forest lands	1.9%
Urban tree planting	1.2%
Improved public transport	0.3%
TOTAL	**22.1%**

Various measures have been suggested which would enable the USA to reduce substantially its emissions of carbon dioxide

(Source: National Defense Council)

new power station it is cheaper for the company to give free insulation and fluorescent light bulbs to the homes and factories in the city that use their electricity. Instead of increasing the supply, they reduce the demand, and save money.

Saving energy is the best and easiest way to slow down the greenhouse warming of the globe. If there really is a need for new power stations, there are other alternatives to fossil fuel and to nuclear power. 'Wind farms', with modern windmills generating electricity, wave power, and power from

Modern windmills   *(© Alex Bartel / Science Photo Library)*

tidal barrages or reservoirs are all good options that are now taken more seriously than they were a few years ago. Such 'renewable' energy has another great advantage over fossil fuel – once you have built the windmills, or hydroelectric plants, the power itself is more or less free.

Even fossil fuel can be used more efficiently. With a traditional, large power station less than half of the energy released by burning the coal or oil gets used as electricity. A lot of the energy disappears as heat up the chimneys or cooling towers of the power station. This heat cannot easily be used, because traditional power stations are usually far away from factories and homes. But if smaller power stations are built nearer to the communities they serve, the waste heat can be piped into the buildings for central heat-ing or to make hot water. Such systems are known as 'combined heat and power'.

THE OTHER HALF OF THE PROBLEM

But remember that although it is still the biggest single contribution to the problem, carbon dioxide is not the only greenhouse gas we have to worry about. Adding in the other greenhouse gases as well, the problem is twice as bad as it would be if we only had carbon dioxide to worry about. How can we begin to tackle the other half of the problem?

The simplest thing that governments could do to slow global warming is to ban the use of CFCs, the gases that are so good at trapping heat (10,000 times better than carbon dioxide) and which also destroy the ozone layer.

Although there is an agreement by many countries to cut back the use of CFCs, even the countries that have signed the agreement are still allowed to manufacture these gases until the end of this century. Many countries have not even signed the agreement. By banning CFCs now, we could possibly delay the amount of warming that would have happened by 2030 until 2040.

Banning CFCs ought to be easy, because these gases are not essential for our way of life. Most people use machines run by electricity and vehicles that run on petrol in their everyday lives, so carbon dioxide will always be released into the air. But we could manage quite well without spray cans, and with a different liquid in the pipes of our refrigerators.

The snag is that it costs money to build the factories to make refrigerators that can use the alternative liquids. Many countries cannot afford to change their factories, but they need refrigerators. This means that change will only happen if rich countries help to pay for it. But this would probably be cheaper for them than paying for the consequences of letting the greenhouse effect grow unchecked.

Other precautions against the release of CFCs cost less. Foamed plastics could be made with bubbles that do not contain CFCs (some already are); computer chips and circuits could be cleaned with different

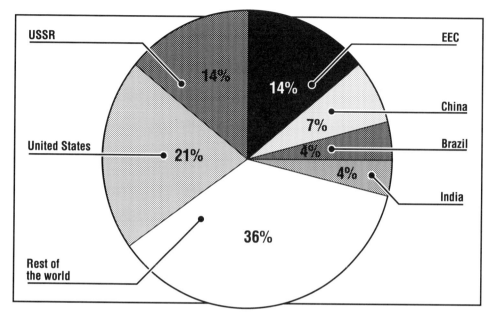

USSR 14%

EEC 14%

China 7%

Brazil 4%

India 4%

United States 21%

Rest of the world 36%

The contribution of different regions of the world to global warming in the 1980s (Source: US Environmental Protection Agency)

solvents. It has even been found that, in some cases, water may work perfectly well.

Banning CFCs is such a straightforward option that it provides a test of our concern about the greenhouse effect. If governments cannot agree on even this simple step, then there is little hope that they will agree on things like using energy more efficiently, and helping lower-income countries with their debt problems.

Methane is more of a problem than CFCs because, just as we cannot imagine a world without electricity, so we cannot imagine making do, worldwide, with less food. But something can be done to reduce the size of the methane problem. Remember that each molecule of methane is twenty times more efficient than a molecule of carbon dioxide at trapping heat. So, even though burning methane produces carbon dioxide, it is still a good idea to burn methane wherever and whenever possible.

This includes methane from rubbish tips and infill sites. Even if it can't be used to generate power, the methane should be burnt off to reduce the growth of the greenhouse effect – and to reduce the chance of an explosion from a build-up of gas. Methane produced by farming activity, especially from cow dung, can be used as a fuel. This helps in two ways. By converting the methane into carbon dioxide, this contribution to the greenhouse effect is reduced, and because farmers have methane

to fuel their stoves, they no longer need to burn wood on their cooking fires, which gives a chance for trees to grow in the region.

THE SILVER LINING

Perhaps you have noticed something interesting and important about all of the actions that are necessary in order to slow down the growth of the greenhouse effect. They are all things that it is a good idea to do anyway!

We should use energy as efficiently as possible, because one day the coal and oil will run out. And if we use energy efficiently, we will save money. We should recycle things, and consume less, because that way we cause less destruction to the planet. And if we do so, we will have more pleasant surroundings to enjoy. We should walk and cycle more instead of going everywhere by car, in order to keep fit and healthy and have more enjoyable lives. We should help the lower-income countries, not burden them with huge debts and interest charges, to make the world a fairer place. And we should preserve natural forests and wildlife wherever we can, to keep our planet as green and pleasant as possible. If we all help to bring the greenhouse effect under control, we will be saving ourselves from droughts, storms and rising sea level.

In short, it makes sense to be less greedy and more unselfish. These are all things that the 'green' movement encourages us to do anyway, to make the world a better place. The threat of the greenhouse effect provides a warning of just how unpleasant the world may become if we do not take notice of what is happening around us.

And that, perhaps, is the silver lining in the greenhouse cloud. The threat of global warming may be just what we need to make us come to our senses and do all the things we know we ought to be doing anyway.

FURTHER READING

Most of the topics covered in this book are dealt with in more detail in two books by John Gribbin, *Hothouse Earth* (Bantam, 1990) and *Winds of Change* (with Mick Kelly, Headway, 1989). *Turning up the Heat*, by Fred Pearce (Bodley Head, 1989) looks at the greenhouse effect alongside other problems of pollution, such as acid rain. And *The Greenhouse Effect*, by Stewart Boyle and John Ardill (New English Library, 1989) goes into a lot more detail on how to save the planet.

If you want to know more about the greenhouse effect in particular, and environmental problems in general, the following books will be useful. Some will be available at bookshops, others through your local library.

John Button, *How to be Green*, Century Hutchinson, 1989

Earth Works Group, *50 Simple Things You Can Do to Save the Earth*, New English Library, 1990

John Elkington and Julia Hailes, *The Green Consumer Guide*, Gollancz, 1988

FoE, *Friends of the Earth Handbook*, Macdonald Optima, 1990

John Gribbin (Editor), *The Breathing Planet*, Blackwell, 1986

Martin Ince, *The Rising Seas*, Earthscan, 1990

Jeremy Leggett (Editor), *Global Warming: The Greenpeace Report*, Oxford University Press, 1990

Jonathon Porritt, *Where on Earth are we Going?*, BBC Books, 1990

Lloyd Timberlake, *Only One Earth*, BBC Books, 1987

The following books are intended especially for younger readers:

Ed Catherall, *Exploring Weather*, Wayland, 1990

John Elkington and Julia Hailes, *The Young Green Consumer Guide*, Gollancz, 1990

Steve Parker, *Weather*, Kingfisher, 1990

Debbie Silver & Bernadette Valley, *The Young Person's Guide to Saving the Planet*, Virago, 1990

Richard Spurgeon, *Ecology*, Usborne, 1988

To play a more active part in saving the planet from human folly you should join an environmental group where you will also be able to get more information about these problems. Here are some useful contact addresses:

Friends of the Earth
26–28 Underwood Street
London N1 7GH

Greenpeace
Canonbury Villas
London N1 2PN

Worldwide Fund for Nature (WWF)
Panda House
Wayside Park
Godalming
Surrey GU7 1XR

Association for the Conservation of Energy (ACE)
9 Sherlock Mews
London W1M 3RH

INDEX